YOUR FAMILY TREE

Using Your Research

by Jim Ollhoff

Visit us at
www.abdopublishing.com

Published by ABDO Publishing Company, 8000 West 78th Street, Suite 310, Edina, MN 55439.
Copyright ©2011 by Abdo Consulting Group, Inc. International copyrights reserved in all countries. No part of this book may be reproduced in any form without written permission from the publisher. ABDO & Daughters™ is a trademark and logo of ABDO Publishing Company.

Printed in the United States of America, North Mankato, Minnesota
052010
092010

 PRINTED ON RECYCLED PAPER

Editor: John Hamilton
Graphic Design: Sue Hamilton
Cover Design: John Hamilton
Cover Photo: iStockphoto
Interior Photos: Alamy-pg 27; Ancestry.com-pgs 6, 8, 10 & 12; Church of Jesus Christ of Latter-Day Saints-pg 11; Denny Orson-pg 26; Getty-pg 9; Granger Collection-pg 16; iStockphoto-pgs 1, 3 & 23; Library of Congress-pgs 7, 14, 15, 17, 18, 19, 22 & 24; Michigan Courts-pg 20; Photo Researchers-pg 29; RavenFire Media-pg 28; Thinkstock-pgs 4, 5, 13 & 21.

Library of Congress Cataloging-in-Publication Data

Ollhoff, Jim, 1959-
  Using your research / Jim Ollhoff.
    p. cm. -- (Your family tree)
  Includes index.
  ISBN 978-1-61613-465-5
  I. Title.
  CS15.5.O49 2010
  929'.1072--dc22
                    2009050805

Contents

Evaluating the Information

Below: How did you get to be you? In many ways, your parents, grandparents, and great-grandparents made you who you are.

When you start researching your family tree, you will collect a lot of information. The longer you research, the more data you will have. Soon, you will be up to your ears in research information, and a lot of it will be confusing and conflicting.

For example, was Great-Grandpa Farnsworth born in 1880, as his gravestone says? Or was he born in 1875, the date on his birth certificate? Or was he born in 1885, which is what the census reports? You have to find ways to sort it all out.

Conflicting information is a natural part of genealogical research. People make mistakes when they record names and dates. The mistakes will be there. It's up to you to evaluate what information is correct, or maybe just figure out what is most likely. That's a big part of what genealogists must do. They must evaluate and use information well.

FRANKLIN
FARNSWORTH
BORN: 1880
DIED: 1918
RIP

Above: The longer you collect family tree information, the more data you will have.

Names

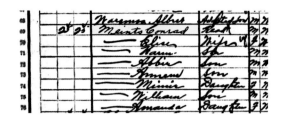

Right: It may be difficult to trace family members when their names have been spelled differently in various documents, such as censuses.

One of the biggest frustrations for genealogical researchers is names. You'll probably discover that your ancestors' names are spelled many different ways. This makes evaluating genealogical information much more difficult.

Toward the end of the 1800s, people started spelling names consistently. It became important to "spell my name correctly." However, before that time, people often didn't care how their names were spelled. They tended to spell words the way they sounded, which meant that names could be spelled many different ways. For example, *Conrad Meints* might be spelled Konrat Myantz, Konrad Mience, or Canrod Moints. It can make genealogical work a challenge.

This problem got worse when people spoke different languages. A census taker might not have known the language an immigrant was speaking, and took a guess on what the immigrant was saying. An entirely new spelling might have been created.

Fortunately, there is a tool that can help. Many genealogical search engines have a tool called "Soundex." This is software that gives you a list of possible spellings for a particular name. You can search all the spellings if you wish. This muddies the water a bit, but you might discover an ancestor or long-lost cousin.

Above: A 1920 census taker fills in family information. By this time, many people cared how their names were spelled, but earlier census takers often spelled names the way they sounded. This resulted in many different spellings of the same family name.

Another problem is penmanship. Sometimes census takers and other document writers had great penmanship. Other times, you can barely make out their handwriting. Further, the handwriting is often in old-fashioned cursive, which is unfamiliar to many people today. This problem can be made even more difficult by the indexer. An indexer works for a company like Ancestry.com, putting genealogical records online. The indexer has to scan the original document and then type into a database what the original document says. Usually, indexers are very good at reading difficult or messy penmanship, but sometimes they get it wrong.

As you evaluate names, remember that people sometimes went by different names. It wasn't uncommon to use their middle name instead of their first name. Sometimes they changed their name if they wanted to hide their past, or were wanted for a crime. As you seek and evaluate names, keep an open mind about how your ancestors might have used their names.

Also, don't forget one important rule: sometimes people share the same name. Let's say you are looking in the census and find a person with the same name as your great-great-grandfather, in the same county where he was born. You can't assume that it's your great-great-grandfather. It might be, but you can't be 100 percent certain until you find more evidence.

Below: Can you read all the names on this 1920 United States census sheet? Sometimes it is very difficult to tell what was written.

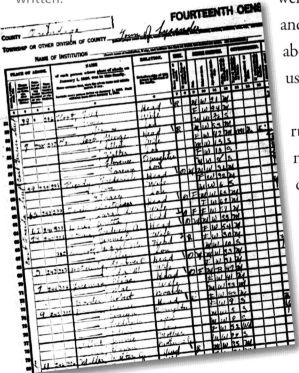

Above: Census takers sometimes had to write while standing up, and in all weather. It is sometimes difficult to read a census taker's writing.

Online Searching

O ne of the biggest sources of online genealogical records is Ancestry.com. They've indexed hundreds of different kinds of documents, including censuses, immigration records, and cemetery records. They have records from other countries, information from each state, and records from individual cities. Their databases grow every day. Subscribers can submit their own family trees to the database, so it's possible that you can find someone else who is researching a part of your family. Ancestry.com is a subscription site, meaning it costs money for each month that you use it. Their Web site is:

www.Ancestry.com

Libraries sometime subscribe to the service, so you may be able to use it there for free.

Left: The home page of Ancestry.com.

Another genealogical gold mine is the website of the Church of Jesus Christ of Latter-Day Saints. They have been indexing genealogical records for many years. They have collected a huge number of files. All of these records are free. No subscription is required. Many of the records are submitted by users, so be cautious not to believe everything you discover. Their Web site is:

www.familysearch.org

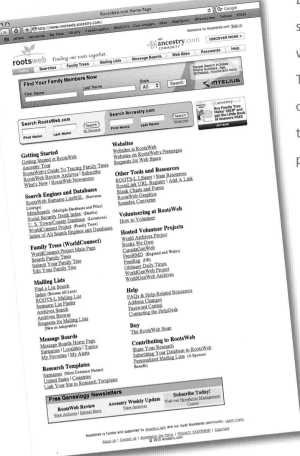

Left: The RootsWeb site is affiliated with Ancestry.com. This Web site can direct you to resources in a particular county.

Another great series of sites is called RootsWeb, which are affiliated with Ancestry.com. These sites can direct you to resources in a particular county. Information might include how to get a vital record, biographies, histories of the county, cemetery locations, or any number of things. The sites are usually run by volunteers, so they vary in the amount of material that is available. To find a particular site, go to a search engine and type RootsWeb and the county and state that you want to search.

There are many free genealogy websites and discussion boards where people post questions, announce findings, and look for information on long-lost cousins. Many people post information about their families. Some of it is good information and some of it is incorrect.

There are also many people trying to make money from genealogical researchers. They might offer to sell you CDs or books with the names of your ancestors and family members. Many times, all they really include is a list of names from the phone book. Some organizations will send you a birth or death certificate, but it will cost you 10 times more than if you did the paperwork yourself. Some people will offer to sell you a family crest, or your complete family history, or the origin of your family. Beware of these scams!

Above: Many people try to make money on genealogy research. Watch out for scams!

Cheats, Liars, and Horse Thieves

Every family has them. You'll eventually find someone in your family tree who was in jail, had children out of wedlock, or perhaps someone who abandoned his or her family.

What would happen if your relatives found out that your Great-Grandpa Ebenezer, the hero of the family, was really a horse thief? That's a difficult question. You'll have to decide whether to share the information or not. In some situations, the darker side of the family history might be better left untold.

On the other hand, even dark family history is still family history. The rich diversity of personalities in a family tree helps make us who we are. Yes, there were some cheats, liars, and horse thieves. There were also some heroes and people who overcame great obstacles. And sometimes the cheats and the heroes are the same people. We are all the product of many circumstances, and the descendants of many kinds of people. Sometimes, we should simply embrace the bad as well as the good.

Below: Whether your family member was a horse thief or a horse trainer, it's important to learn about the bad as well as the good.

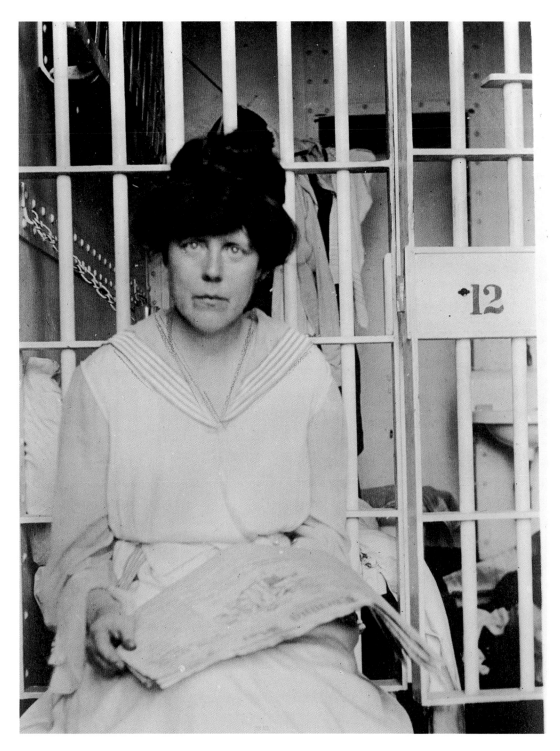

Above: In 1917, suffragette Lucy Burns was arrested and sent to jail while campaigning for women's rights. Some thought she was a villain, while others said she was a hero.

Social History

Once you get your ancestors placed into a time and a country, it can be fun to read up on the history of that country. For example, if your Great-Great-Grandmother Molly O'Donnell was born in 1830 in Ireland, you might learn something about her by reading about what was going on in Ireland at that time.

Historical facts can also give you some clues about why your ancestors left their home countries when they did. Immigration history reveals that many people often left a country at the same time. Sometimes crop failures caused terrible hardships. Insects or drought could wreak havoc on farm fields. Sometimes persecution caused people to leave, or people left to escape military service. Sometimes people left because of overcrowding or poverty. The promise of cheap land in America was a powerful attraction to these people.

Right: Ireland's great potato famine in the 1800s caused the country's population to decrease steadily. Thousands died of starvation or left the country.

Above: An Irish farm family. A plant disease destroyed most of Ireland's potato crop in the mid-1800s. The great potato famine caused starvation and death to thousands of Irish people. Thousands more chose to leave Ireland and immigrate to America and other countries.

Nebraska farmer and family, 1886

Colorado teacher and students, 1915

Nebraska hardware store, 1886

Georgia doctor, 1889

It's important to separate facts from hunches. For example, you know your Great-Great-Grandmother Molly O'Donnell came to the United States in 1846. You also know there was a huge exodus from Ireland because of potato crop failures beginning in 1845. But you can't say for sure that Molly came here because of crop failures, unless you have letters or a diary from her stating that fact. However, you can say, "It's possible that Molly came to this country from Ireland because the area she came from suffered crop failures at the time of her immigration."

It's fun to read what everyday life was like for your ancestors. Politics change, a country's governmental officials come and go, but farmers tend their farm no matter who is in charge. What was it like to be a farmer in that country at that time? Or a teacher? Or a merchant? Or a medical doctor? It can be very informative to learn about the lives of regular people. Studying daily life is called "social history."

HARPER'S WEEKLY.

A JOURNAL OF CIVILIZATION

Vol. XXIV.—No. 1209.]   NEW YORK, SATURDAY, FEBRUARY 28, 1880.   [SINGLE COPIES TEN CENTS.
[$4.00 PER YEAR IN ADVANCE.

Entered according to Act of Congress, in the Year 1880, by Harper & Brothers, in the Office of the Librarian of Congress, at Washington.

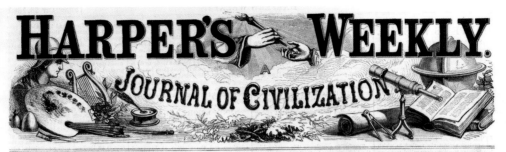

It's possible your Irish relative came to America in the mid-1800s to escape the potato famine. The only way to know for sure is if there are letters or a diary entry stating that fact.

THE *HERALD* OF RELIEF FROM AMERICA.

Family Trees and Adoption

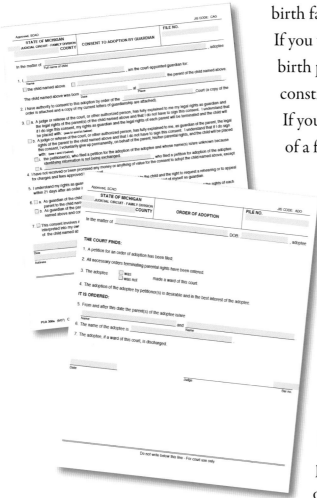

If you are adopted, then you have some options for your family tree. Your first choice is to decide whether to do the family tree of your birth family or your adoptive family. If you want the family tree to be a birth pedigree, you might want to construct the tree of your birth family. If you want genealogy to be more of a family history, then you might want to do your adoptive family. You can certainly do both families, but that's a lot more work.

Finding your birth family might be difficult or almost impossible. Searching for them can be frustrating because of adoption laws, and it can also be emotionally tiring. It might be rewarding to find your birth parents, or emotionally difficult, or both.

Above: If you are adopted, you can do a family tree of your birth family or your adoptive family, or both.

If you choose to try to find your birth parents, you should start with your adoptive parents. They may have clues, adoption documents, perhaps even the names of your birth parents. The adoption agency might have information, but they may not be able to tell you much. The laws allowing agencies to share information is different from state to state. Policies of various adoption agencies vary, too. There is a complex web of laws and policies you may have to deal with. Some states have mutual consent registries or reunion registries. These help children and their birth parents find each other. Internet groups and mailing lists might also be able to help.

As you construct your family tree, it is not unusual to run across adoption among your ancestors. In previous generations, adoption was often informal, with little or no documentation. In the 1930s and afterward, governments began to pass laws governing adoption, and requiring confidentiality.

It was not uncommon for a family to take in a grandchild or a relative's child who could no longer be cared for. As you research your ancestors, you might get clues about this. For example, you might notice a child in the family with a different last name. Sometimes, in previous generations, it is simply not possible to tell whether it is a birth child or an adopted child.

Below: In the past, adoption was often informal. It was not uncommon for a grandparent to raise a grandchild or another relative's child.

Above: To find birth parents, it's a good idea to start by talking to adoptive parents.

They may have some information, perhaps even the birth parents' names.

Tips for Success

Below: In genealogical research, be sure to question all of your information. Write down who said what, and where the information came from.

The biggest tip for success at this stage in your genealogical research is to be suspicious of every piece of information you find. Make sure you write down who said what, and where you got the information. If you find a census that says Great-Grandpa Mulligan was born in 1898, make sure you record which census said that. As unbelievable as it seems, birthdates might change from census to census. Never underestimate the chances of human error occurring! Write down your source of every piece of information, as in Example 1 (page 25).

24

Great-Grandpa Harry Mulligan

Born: 1898 (according to the 1900 census)

1889 (according to the 1910 census)

1889 (according to the 1944 obituary in the
Los Angeles Times newspaper)

Born in Ireland (city unknown), (according to the 1900, 1910,
and 1920 censuses)

Immigrated: Arrived in New York on January 27, 1920 (according to
the passenger lists from the steamship *Celeste*)

Lived: According to Grandma Bertha Jenkins, Great-Grandpa Mulligan
got on a train in New York after getting off the steamship and went
immediately to Los Angeles. However, I have a 1921 deed of sale for 15
acres of land in Sheridan County, Kansas. Did he stop in Kansas and farm
for a few years?

Married: March 3, 1925, in Los Angeles, to Marie Whiteneck

Children: Vinnie, born July 3, 1926

Bertha, born October 2, 1928

Occupation: Shoemaker (according to the 1925 city directory)

Died: March 29, 1945, of heart failure (according to the death certificate)

March 28, 1945 (according to the tombstone)

March 27, 1945 (according to the Social Security death records)

Example 1

You will find information that is strange, wrong, or doesn't seem to fit. Part of the fun of genealogical research is to be a detective, trying to figure out which clues are right and which clues are wrong.

Another tip for success is to make a trip to the town where your ancestors lived, if possible. Check out the public library and the county historical society. Many times, they have history books of that county. They may have biographies of prominent citizens. They might have material in archives or on microfilm that is not available online.

Below: A county historical society is an excellent place to research a person's ancestors.

Above: Many public libraries have records in their archives or on microfilm.

What's Next?

Below: A news clipping is an example of an informal document. It may be more trustworthy than the family history that gets passed down by word of mouth.

So, you've got a family tree. You've collected a lot of information about where people came from, who married who, and who their children are. You've evaluated the information and recorded where it came from. What's next?

The next step is to collect more primary documents. These are the sources written when a person was alive, including birth and marriage certificates, and many other kinds of documents. Some of these documents are formal and official, like birth certificates. Other kinds of documents are informal, like obituaries and news clippings. These documents can provide a huge amount of information that is usually more trustworthy than the family history that gets passed down by word of mouth.

Future genealogical steps might also include looking at the history of immigration of your ancestors. Another step might even include a DNA test. You are well on your way to creating a family tree that will give a great picture of your ancestry!

Above: A DNA test may help you look at the history of immigration of your ancestors.

Glossary

ANCESTORS

The people from whom you are directly descended. Usually this refers to people in generations prior to your grandparents.

ANCESTRY.COM

A massive series of databases for genealogical research. It is a subscription site, which means you have to pay to use it. Some libraries subscribe to the site, so you may be able to use it for free. Check with your local library.

FAMILY CREST

Also called a coat of arms. During the Middle Ages, a graphic design created for a specific individual. A crest was not passed down, nor was it connected to a family surname.

FAMILY TREE

A way of showing you, your parents, grandparents, and previous generations.

FAMILYSEARCH.ORG

A free website run by the Church of Jesus Christ of Latter-Day Saints. It provides a huge database of genealogical materials.

GENEALOGY

The study of your ancestors and your family history.

Middle Ages

In European history, the Middle Ages were a period defined by historians as roughly between 476 AD and 1450 AD.

Primary Documents

A primary document is something created by an eyewitness to an event, someone who was there when the event happened. It can be an official document, like a birth certificate, or it can simply be a journal or letter written by an eyewitness. The sooner the document is created after the event, the better.

RootsWeb

A volunteer-run series of websites on the county level that posts genealogical material about that county.

Social History

The history that explores the daily life of regular people.

Soundex

Software that will help you spell a name in different ways, so it is easier to search all the possible spellings.

Suffragette

A woman who fought for women's rights. American suffragettes influenced the passing of the 19th Amendment to the United States Constitution in 1920. This gave women the right to vote.

Surname

A person's last name.

Index

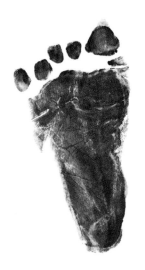
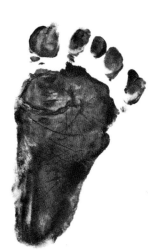